Amazing Math Puzzles

Adam Hart-Davis
Illustrated by Jeff S⋯⋯

Sterling Publishing Co., Inc.
New York

To my dear old dad

Many thanks to all those who have inspired my
interest in math: from my first math teacher, Mr.
Turner, to Archimedes, Eratosthenes, Diophantus,
Ian Stewart, and David Wells.

Edited by Claire Bazinet

Library of Congress Cataloging-in-Publication Data

Hart-Davis, Adam.
   Amazing math puzzles / by Adam Hart-Davis;
illustrated by Jeff Sinclair.
     p.   cm.
     Includes index.
     ISBN 0-8069-9667-6
     1. Mathematical recreations. I. Title.
   QA95.H352   1998
   793.7´4–dc21   98-3367
                                                                    CIP

10 9 8 7 6 5 4 3 2 1

Published by Sterling Publishing Company, Inc.
387 Park Avenue South, New York, N.Y. 10016
© 1998 by Adam Hart-Davis
Distributed in Canada by Sterling Publishing
℅ Canadian Manda Group, One Atlantic Avenue, Suite 105
Toronto, Ontario, Canada M6K 3E7
Distributed in Great Britain and Europe by Cassell PLC
Wellington House, 125 Strand, London WC2R 0BB, England
Distributed in Australia by Capricorn Link (Australia) Pty Ltd.
P.O. Box 6651, Baulkham Hills, Business Centre,
NSW 2153, Australia
Manufactured in the United States of America
All rights reserved

Sterling ISBN 0-8069-9667-6

Contents

Index 95

Introduction

The old Arab lay dying, so he called in his three sons. "My boys," he said, "I shall soon be gone, so I leave to you my camels. But," a strange gleam coming into his eye, "you must divide them up as I say, in a mathematical way. To Abdul, my firstborn son, I leave exactly half my camels; to Saleem, my second son, I leave one quarter of them; and to Yussuf, my youngest, I leave one fifth. Now go, and make the most of your inheritance." Then, at peace, he closed his eyes and died.

Later, when the sons went out to the compound and counted their father's camels, they found that there were nineteen. Eager to follow the wishes of their father, they began to work out their shares. Suddenly, in a shocked voice, Abdul said, "I can't have half the camels. Half of 19 is 9½. I don't want to cut a camel in half!"

Saleem was also unhappy. "If I take a quarter, that makes 4¾ camels, and I certainly don't want to cut away a quarter of a camel!" Yussuf, the youngest, was even more upset, because his inheritance would be only 3⅘ camels–and it looked like most would be in pieces!

They all sat and stared at the camels, sorely troubled.

Finally, along came their old uncle Isaac, leading his tired old camel Fatimah; she was coughing, and lame, and covered with sores, but he loved her dearly. Seeing their faces, "What is wrong, boys?" he asked. The sons told him what their father had said on his deathbed, and that they now had no idea what to do.

Uncle Isaac smiled at the boys' dilemma. "As your father would surely have wished," he said, handing over the rope lead, "take Fatima and add her to the herd."

"We couldn't possibly take your camel," they protested politely, really horrified at the thought of such a diseased old fleabag among their smart young animals. But old uncle Isaac insisted, pushing the stumbling Fatimah among the glossy camels of the herd. "Now work out your sums," he said.

"But we've tried and tried," they said, all together, "and it doesn't work out without cutting up the camels!"

"Ah, my nephews, that was true with 19 camels, but now there are 20 camels in the herd. Try again."

So they did. Abdul was pleased to work out that one half of 20 is 10 camels; he quickly went into the compound and chose the ten strongest and most beautiful animals, leaving 10 camels in the compound.

Saleem had quickly calculated that one quarter of 20 was 5; so he bounced in and took the five best camels there, leaving 5 for Yussuf to choose from.

Yussuf knew one fifth of 20 is 4; so he took the four best camels left to him. Then there was just one camel in the compound—poor old Fatimah. Wise Isaac came and led Fatimah away, leaving all his brother's sons happy with their inheritances.

* * *

Why do you think Fatimah made such a difference? Puzzling, isn't it? That's what this book is about—puzzling math. Most of the pages in the book hold only one puzzle, with the answer upside-down in a box at the bottom of the following page. But don't peek until you have tried your best to think out the answer. A few puzzles have a little hint to help you, too. When you are able to work out an answer to a puzzle, you will feel great.

The puzzles on the lefthand pages are mostly easier; try them first, then go on to the tougher ones on the right side.

Good luck!

The Puzzles

Sox Unseen

Sam's favorite colors are blue and green, so it's not surprising that he has six blue sox and six green sox in his sock drawer. Unfortunately, they are hopelessly mixed up and one day, in complete darkness, he has to grab some sox to wear.

How many sox does he have to take from the drawer to make sure he gets a matching pair—either green or blue? (For some strange reason, his mother insists that his socks have to match!)

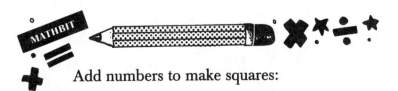

Add numbers to make squares:

1=	$1 = 1×1$
1+**2**+1=	$4 = 2×2$
1+2+**3**+2+1=	$9 = 3×3$
1+2+3+**4**+3+2+1=	$16 = 4×4$
1+2+3+4+**5**+4+3+2+1=	$25 = 5×5$
1+2+3+4+5+**6**+5+4+3+2+1=	$36 = 6×6$
1+2+3+4+5+6+**7**+6+5+4+3+2+1=	$49 = 7×7$

Gloves Galore!

Gloria's favorite colors are pink and yellow. She has sox in those colors, of course, but she *really* likes gloves!

In her glove drawer, there are six pairs of pink gloves and six pairs of yellow gloves, but like Sam's sox, the gloves are all mixed up. In complete darkness, how many gloves does Gloria have to take from the drawer in order to be sure she gets one pair? She doesn't mind whether it's a pink or yellow pair.

(Hint: This may sound a bit like Sox Unseen, *but watch out! Gloves are more complicated than sox.)*

Sox Unseen

Sam has to take out 3 sox; then he's bound to get two of the same color.

Birthday Hugs

"O frabjous day! Calloo Callay!"*
> It's Jenny's birthday!

Jenny invites her three best friends Janey, Jeannie, and Joany to come to a party at her house, and when they all arrive they all give each other hugs.

How many hugs is that altogether?

*A special "gold star" if you can name the work and author of this famous line.

The last joint of your thumb is probably close to an inch long, measuring from nail to knuckle. The spread from the tip of your thumb to the tip of your forefinger is probably five or six inches. Measure them with a ruler—then you can use these "units" to measure the lengths of all sorts of things.

SOLUTION

Gloves Galore!

This is trickier than the sox, because some gloves fit on the right hand and some on the left. You *might* pick out all 12 left hand gloves, one right after the other, but then the next must make a pair; so you need to take 13 gloves to make sure.

Sticky Shakes

For John's birthday celebration, he invites six friends—Jack, Jake, Jim, Joe, Julian, and Justin—to a favorite burger place where they order thick and sticky milk shakes: banana, chocolate, maple, peanut butter, pineapple, strawberry, and vanilla.

While they slurp the shakes, their hands get sticky. Laughing about "shake" hands, they decide to actually do it—shake hands with their shake-sticky hands. So each boy shakes hands once with everyone else. How many handshakes is that altogether?

Birthday Hugs

Each girl kisses 3 others; so it looks like 4 × 3 = 12 kisses, but that would be counting Jenny kissing Janey as one kiss, and Janey kissing Jenny as another, counting each kiss twice. Actually, there are six kisses altogether.

Gold Star answer: Jabberwocky *by Lewis Carroll.*

The Wolf, the Goat, and the Cabbage

You are traveling through difficult country, taking with you a wolf, a goat, and a cabbage. All during the trip the wolf wants to eat the goat, and the goat wants to eat the cabbage, and you have to be careful to prevent either calamity.

You come to a river and find a boat which can take you across, but it's so small that you can take only one passenger at a time—either the wolf, or the goat, or the cabbage.

You must never leave the wolf alone with the goat, nor the goat alone with the cabbage.

So how can you get them all across the river?

Sticky Shakes

21.

Same trick as with the kisses. Either you can say each of the 7 shakes with six; so the total is a half of 7 × 6, or 21 shakes. Or you can say John shakes with 6; Jack shakes with 5 others (don't count John again); Jake shakes with 4 others, and so on. The total number of handshakes is 6 + 5 + 4 + 3 + 2 + 1 = 21.

Floating Family

Mom and Dad and two kids have to cross a river, and they find a boat, but it is so small it can carry only one adult or two kids. Luckily both the kids are good rowers, but how can the whole family get across the river?

MATHBIT

Did you know that most drinking glasses and cups have a circumference greater than their height? Test it out on some you have at home.

Take a piece of string and wrap it carefully once around a glass. You will almost always find the string is longer than the height of the glass. When is this not true?

Now you can amaze your friends by predicting this fun mathematical fact with one of their glasses before you measure it!

SOLUTION

The Wolf, the Goat, and the Cabbage

Take the goat across. Go back; take the wolf across, and bring the goat back. Take the cabbage across. Go back for the goat. Then the goat is never alone with either the wolf or the cabbage.

Slippery Slopes

Brenda the Brave sets off to climb a mountain which is 12,000 feet high. She plans to climb 3000 feet each day, before taking overnight rests. A mischievous mountain spirit, however, decides to test Brenda's resolve. Each night, Brenda's sleeping bag, with her soundly asleep in it, is magically moved 2000 feet *back down* the mountain, so that when Brenda awakes in the morning she finds herself only 1000 feet higher than she was the morning before!

Not one to give up, Brenda eventually succeeds. But how many days does it take her to reach the summit?

The Long and the Short of the Grass

Mr. Greengrass wants his lawn to be tidy and likes the grass cut short. Because he doesn't like mowing but wants to be able sit outside and read the paper on Sunday mornings and be proud of the smooth lawn, he decides to hire some good young mowers.

Two kids agree to mow Mr. Greengrass's grass on Saturdays for 15 weeks. To make sure they come every single Saturday, he agrees to pay them, at the end of the 15 weeks, $2 for every week that they mow it—as long as they will give him $3 for every week they miss.

At the end of the 15 weeks, they owe him exactly as much as he owes them, which is good news for Mr. Greengrass, but a rotten deal for the kids! How many weeks did they miss?

MATHBIT

When drawing a graph, some people can never remember which is the x-axis and which is the y-axis. Here's a neat way to remember: say to yourself, "x is *a cross*."

SOLUTION

Slippery Slopes

Ten days. After 9 days and 9 nights, she is at 9000 feet. On the 10th day she climbs 3000 feet to the summit!

Nine Coins

Wendy got into trouble in her math class. She was sorting out money she planned to spend after school, and accidentally dropped nine coins on the floor. They fell with such a clatter that the teacher was angry at the disturbance and told Wendy to remain at her desk after school until she could arrange all nine coins on the desktop in at least six rows with three coins in each row.

Can you do it?

Wendy did. In fact she did even better. She arranged her nine coins in no less than *ten* rows, with three in each row! Her teacher was quite impressed.

Can you make ten rows?

Remember pi to five decimal places by counting the number of letters in each word in the following question:

CAN I FIND A SMART PINEAPPLE?   (Pi = 3.14159)

The Long and the Short of the Grass

They mowed the grass on 9 Saturdays, earning 9 × $2 = $18, and missed 6 Saturdays, losing 6 × $3 = $18.

Eight Coins

Here's a really neat puzzle that you can use to baffle your friends. Once you learn the secret, it's easy, but if you don't know the secret, the puzzle is quite hard. Still, you just might luck into it, so why not try your hand before you look at the answer.

First you have to make a line of 8 coins on the table, like this:

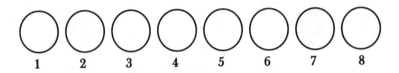

Pick one coin, jump it over two others, and put it on top of the third. The challenge is to finish with four piles of two coins after only four moves.

(Hint: It's simply a matter of knowing which move to make right at the start.)

Nine Coins

She set up the coins as shown.
Can you find the rows now?
Lets count them.
The 3-coin rows are:
3 rows across (top, middle and bottom), 4 diagonal (two one way, two the other, 1 down the middle, and...
...2 *long* diagonals criss-crossing through the center!

Tricky Connections

Three new houses (below) have been built along a highway in Alaska. Each house needs an electricity supply and a water supply; however the permafrost means nothing can be buried underground, and no supply must ever cross a driveway. Too, a new safety law states that no electricity supply may cross a water pipeline.

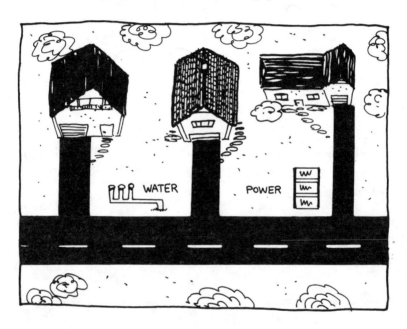

Can the houses be connected up?

SOLUTION

Eight Coins

The secret is to start with #4 and move it onto #7—or start with #5 and move it onto #2. Then it's reasonably easy; try it and see. (If you want the whole solution: move #4 to #7, #6 to #2, #1 to #3, and #5 to #8.)

Odd Balls

Lucky you! You have nine tennis balls...

...and four shopping bags.

Your challenge is to put all the balls in the bags in such a way that there is an odd number of balls in each bag? That is, each bag must contain 1, 3, 5, 7, or 9 balls.

Can it be done?

(Hint: Yes, it can, but there's a trick to it!)

Challenge your friends to write down the largest possible number using only two digits. They'll probably write 99, but then you can top them.

The correct answer is 9^9, which means $9 \times 9 \times 9 \times 9 \times 9 \times 9 \times 9 \times 9 \times 9$, or 387,420,489 (nearly four hundred million)!

SOLUTION

Tricky Connections

No, it can't be done. The connections are impossible without allowing one line to cross another, using a bridge, or by putting a line under a house!

For a little change of pace...

Mirror writing is writing you can hardly read unless you use a mirror to turn it back to front, like this:

Mirror writing is writing you can hardly read unless you use a mirror to turn it back to front, like this:

Some people can write ordinary writing with their right hand and mirror writing with their left hand...at the same time!

Try mirror writing yourself.

In the meantime, try to see if you can read this mirror-writing paragraph *without a mirror:*

Five hundred years ago a brilliant Italian painter and designer called Leonardo da Vinci filled notebooks with drawings and descriptions of wonderful inventions—airplanes, helicopters, pumps, and bicycles. Probably to keep his ideas secret, he wrote all his notes in mirror writing.

Odd Balls

Yes, this can be done, but you have to put at least one bag inside of another. You could put 3 balls in each of 3 bags, and then one of these bags inside the fourth bag. Or you could put all the balls in bag 1, put that in bag 2, put that in bag 3, and put the whole lot in bag 4. And there are many others!

Madam Palindrome

A word with a series of letters reading the same backwards as it does forwards is called a palindrome. MOM is a palindrome. So is DAD, and GOD'S DOG (ignoring the apostrophe).

Palindromes aren't the same as mirror writing, because most letters look strange backwards. MOM looks the same in the mirror, but ɒAɒ looks weird.

Making up palindromes is hard. Longer ones are much harder than short ones and even the best often don't make much sense. Here are some palindrome words; can you find others, or even sentences?

ANNA BOB DEED DID LIL NOON POP RACECAR SIS

The French engineer who first dreamed up a plan to cut through Central America to make the Panama Canal was called Ferdinand de Lesseps. A headline in a newspaper of that time might have said: A MAN, A PLAN, A CANAL, PANAMA!—which is a palindrome.

A town called Yreka in Northern California has four bread shops, but none of them, I am sorry to say, is called YREKA BAKERY, which would be a nifty palindrome.

Now, answer this riddle with a palindrome: How did the first man mentioned in the Bible introduce himself to his wife?

Cube of Cheese

Honoria was hosting a party–entertaining some friends. She had planned a specially elegant dinner, and wanted a cube of cheese as part of an appetizer display.

Looking in the refridgerator, she found she did have some cheese, but it was in the form of a complete sphere; in other words, a ball of cheese. Well, she would simply have to cut a cube of cheese from the cheese ball.

Honoria can't resist a puzzle so she spent most of the time as she prepared dinner wondering how to cut the sphere of cheese into a cube quickly; that is, using the fewest number of cuts.

What is the smallest number of cuts you have to make to cut a cube from a sphere?

Potato Pairs

In Idaho, they proudly say they have giant potatoes, and unusual potato sellers. One of the strangest potato sellers is Potato Mo. She never sells her potatoes one at a time, nor in bags of five or ten pounds. She sells potatoes only in pairs!

One day, Cal the cook wanted a potato that weighed just two pounds, so he went and asked Mo what she had available.

"I have only three potatoes left," she answered. "Here they are: A, B, and C.

"A and B together weigh three pounds; A and C together weigh five pounds; B and C together weigh four pounds. You can have any pair you want."

Can you help Cal the cook buy a pair of potatoes? Which if any of the potatoes weighs two pounds?

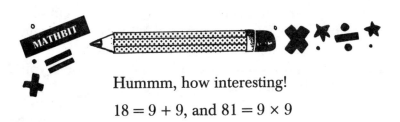

Hummm, how interesting!

$18 = 9 + 9$, and $81 = 9 \times 9$

Sugar Cubes

The Big Sugar Corporation wants to persuade people to use lumps of sugar, or sugar cubes; so they run a puzzle competition. The first person to get the answers right (the puzzle is made up of three parts) wins free sugar for life! Here's the puzzle:

You have been sent a *million cubes* of sugar. Yes, that's right, 1,000,000 sugar cubes! Each cube is just half an inch long, half an inch wide, and half an inch high.

1. Suppose the cubes arrived all wrapped up and packed together into one giant cube. Where could you put it? Under a table? In the garage? Or would you need a warehouse? *(Hint: What you need to work out is, How many little cubes would there be in each direction? And how long, wide and high would the giant cube be?)*

2. Now, suppose you decide to lay the cubes all out in a square on the ground—all packed together but this time only one layer deep? How big a space would you need? Your living room floor? A tennis court? Or would you need a parking lot the size of a city block?

Potato Pairs

Add all the weights together and divide by two to get the total weight of the three potatoes: $(3+5+4)/2 = 6$ pounds. Now, since A and B together weigh 3 pounds, and $A + B + C$ together weigh 6 pounds, then C must weigh 3 pounds. A and C together weigh 5 pounds, which means that A must weigh 2 pounds; so Cal should buy either A and B or A and C.

3. Now for the big one. Pile all the million cubes one on top of the other into a tower just one cube thick. (You'll need *very* steady hands and not a breath of wind!) How high will the pile be? As high as a house (say 25 feet)? As high as New York's Empire State Building (1472 feet)? As high as Mount Adams (12,000 feet) in Washington state or Mount Everest (29,000 feet)? Or will the pile of cubes reach the moon (240,000 miles)?

See all solutions below.

Sugar Cubes

1. The first trick is to count the zeros! To find out how big the big cube is you need to find the cube root of a million. A million has six zeros—1,000,000—so its cube root must have one third of six—two zeros—100.

The cube root of a million is a hundred. So the big cube is 100 cubes long, 100 wide, and 100 high. Each cube is half an inch; so 100 cubes is 50 inches, or just over 4 feet long. You would not fit this under a table, but it would go easily in a garage.

2. This time you are making a square; so you need the square root of a million. A million has six zeros; its square root must have half six; that is , three zeros—1000. The square root of a million is a thousand. So the big square on the ground is 1000 half inches long and 1000 half inches wide. 1000 half inches is 500 inches; dividing by 12 will give you 41 feet 8 inches. You could fit this square on a tennis court.

3. The pile is a million cubes high; a million half inches, or 500,000 inches. Divide by 12 for 41,666 feet 8 inches. This is higher than Mount Everest. You could make one pile as high as Mount Everest and one as high as Mount Adams, and still have a few cubes left over!

Crackers!

Mad Marty, crazy as crackers, invites his friends to a cracker puzzle party. The puzzle he sets them is this: How many different kinds of spread can you put on a cracker?

Everyone brings a different kind of spread and Marty supplies a gigantic box of crackers. Then they all get down to business:

Marty has a cracker with mayo =   1 spread

Pete brings peanut butter; so now
   they have: (**1**) mayo, (**2**) peanut
   butter, (**3**) mayo and peanut
   butter =   3 spreads

Jake brings jelly; so now they have
   (**1**) mayo, (**2**) peanut butter,
   (**3**) mayo and peanut butter,
   (**4**) jelly, (**5**) jelly and mayo,
   (**6**) jelly and peanut butter,
   (**7**) jelly and mayo and peanut
   butter =   7 spreads

Hank brings honey =   how many
                               spreads?

Charlie brings cheese =   how many
                               spreads?

Fred brings fish-paste =   how many
                               spreads?

Crate Expectations

You have six bottles of pop for a party, and you want to arrange them in an attractive pattern in the crate. Four will make a square...

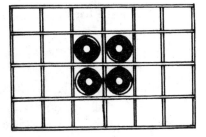

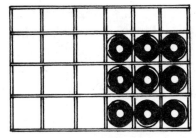

and nine will make a square. But six is a trickier number. How about an even number of bottles in each line?

Can you arrange them so that, in every row and in every column, the number of bottles is even (0, 2, 4, or 6)?

(Hint: This is quite tricky, and fine puzzle to challenge your friends with. A good way to practice is to draw a grid on a piece of paper and use coins instead of bottles.)

Take It Away!

This is a game for two players. You will need someone to play against. It's a simple game, but the winning plan is really cunning. See if you can work it out just by playing the game.

You need about 12 or 15 small things—marbles, cookies, hard candies, pencils. It doesn't matter what they are, as long as they are all roughly the same size. Put them in a pile between the two players.

The first player takes either 1 or 2 things; then the second player takes 1 or 2 things, and they continue playing in this way. The winner is the player who takes the *last* thing.

For example, in a game starting with 14 pencils:

Player A takes 2	leaving 12
Player B takes 2	leaving 10
Player A takes 2	leaving 8
Player B takes 1	leaving 7
Player A takes 1	leaving 6
Player B takes 2	leaving 4
Player A takes 1	leaving 3
Player B takes 1	leaving 2
Player A takes 2 and wins	

OK, try it with a friend.

SOLUTION

Crate Expectations

There are many different patterns
that work, but here is an easy one
to remember.
Now try ten bottles!

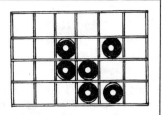

28

Oddwins

Here is another game for two players. You need 11 small objects—cookies, pebbles, paper clips.

Put the pile of objects between the players, and play alternately. First Player A takes either 1 or 2 objects. Then Player B takes 1 or 2 objects. Continue until all the objects have been taken.

The winner is the player who, at the end of the game, has an ODD number of objects—either 5 or 7.

MATHBIT

Most people have a "wingspan" almost exactly equal to their height. So if you are 4 feet 10 inches high, then you will probably find that you measure 4 feet 10 inches from fingertip to fingertip with your arms stretched right out as far as they will go. Get a friend to help you measure your wingspan and check. Then you can use your wingspan as a measuring tool.

SOLUTION

Take It Away

If you are left with 3, you must lose, because you can't take all three, but if you take 1 your opponent will take 2, and if you take 2 your opponent will take 1. So the first rule for winning is, to try to leave your opponent with 3 items! You can also win if you leave 6, because after leaving 6 you can always leave 3 next turn. And you can win if you leave 9. Can you spot the pattern?

Witches' Brew

Three witches were mixing up a dreadful mathematical spell in their cauldron, and one of them–Fat Freddy–was reading out the recipe to the others.

Eye of newt and toe of frog
Wool of bat and tongue of dog

Suddenly they realized they needed some liquid–2 pints of armpit sweat. They had a bucketful of sweat, a saucepan that when full held exactly 3 pints, and a jug that when full held exactly 1 pint. How could they get exactly 2 pints?

(Hint: Try filling the pan, and then filling the jug from it.)

Witches' Stew

Many years later the same witches, now even older and more haggard, were mixing up a super-disgusting stew in their cauldron:

Adder's fork and blind worm's sting
Lizard's leg and howlet's wing...

And once again they needed to add the sweat, mixed this time with tears. They had a bucketful of liquid, and they needed to add exactly 4 pints, but all they had to measure it was a pitcher that held exactly 5 pints and a pot that held exactly 3.

How could they measure out exactly 4 pints?

The Pizza and the Sword

The room is full of hungry people. You have just had delivered a monster pizza, which covers most of the table. It's too hot to touch, but you need to cut it up quickly so that everyone can start eating.

What is the maximum number of pieces you can make with three straight cuts across? You may not move the pieces until you have finished cutting; so you can't pile them on top of one another!

You could make the three cuts side by side, which would give you one extra piece for each cut; so you would get four pieces altogether.

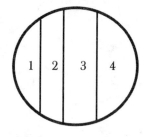

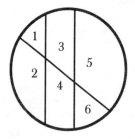

Or, you could make two cuts side by side, and then the third across both of them. That would give you six pieces. But could you make more than six?

(Hint: Nobody said the pieces all have to be the same size; indeed it would be better if they were all different sizes!)

Witches' Stew

Fill the pitcher to the brim. Use it to fill the pot, which leaves just 2 pints in the pitcher. Empty the pot back into the bucket. Pour the 2 pints from the pitcher into the pot. Fill the pitcher again. Now carefully top off the pot from the pitcher. This will take exactly 1 pint, because there are 2 pints in it already. That leaves exactly 4 pints in the pitcher—pour them into the cauldron!

Now, for a 4th cut!

And what if you had time to make a fourth straight cut with your sword? How many extra pieces could you make then?

(Hint: think about how many extra pieces you can make with each cut.)

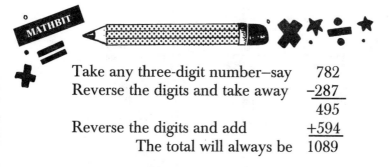

Take any three-digit number—say	782
Reverse the digits and take away	−287
	495
Reverse the digits and add	+594
The total will always be	1089

The *only exception* is that sometimes when you first take away you get 99. You have to treat this as 099. Then when you reverse and add you get 099 + 990, which is equal to 1089!

SOLUTION

The Pizza and the Sword

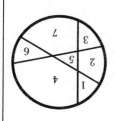

To get the maximum number of pieces you must make sure that each cut crosses all the previous cuts, but not at old crossings. If all three cuts cross in the middle, you can get only 6 pieces, but if you keep the crossings separate you get 7.

Pencil Squares

Lay 15 pencils (or straws, toothpicks or what have you) out on the table to make five equal squares like this:

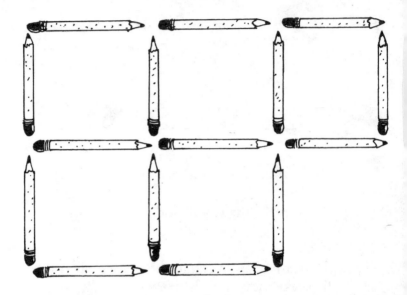

Now take away just three of the pencils, and leave only three squares.

The Pizza and the Sword (4th cut!)

To begin with, the pizza is in 1 piece. With your first cut you make 1 new piece—2 in all. With your 2nd cut, as long as it crosses the first, you make 2 new pieces—4 in all. With your 3rd cut you make 3 new pieces (total 7), and with your 4th cut you make 4 new pieces, for a total of 11 pieces of pizza.

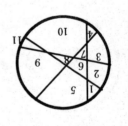

Pencil Triangles

Here's a really tough puzzle that you can use to stump your friends, after you have figured it out. If you are able to solve it without peeking at the solution, you are doing better than a whole lot of brilliant people.

This time, take 6 pencils (or straws or toothpicks) and arrange them so that they form four equal triangles.

MATHBIT

What is wrong with dividing 16 by 64 by crossing out the 6s, like this?

$$\frac{1\cancel{6}}{\cancel{6}4} = \frac{1}{4}$$

Cancelling the 6s in the division 16/64 is wrong because each is only part of a number, and you must always cancel a whole number. Although it seems to work in this case, it's just by luck. (You get into terrible trouble if you cancel, say, the 5s in 15/45; you get 1/4, but the right answer is 1/3!)

SOLUTION

Pencil Squares

From puzzle, remove top middle pencil and two lower-left corner pencils.

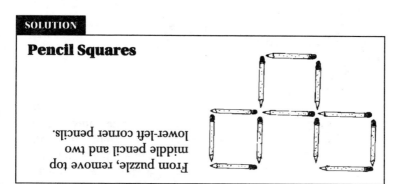

Cyclomania

In the kids' playground, Donna was delighted to find bicycles with two wheels, and tricycles with, of course, three wheels.

They came in all sorts of different shapes and sizes and colors, but she took a count and discovered that they had 12 wheels altogether.

How many bicycles did Donna find there? And how many tricycles?

Here's another puzzle question to stump your pals. How can you make 100 using just four 9s? How?

Answer: 99 9/9

SOLUTION

Pencil Triangles

What you have to do is build them into a 3-dimensional pyramid, with a triangle on each of its three sides, and *one under-neath.*

36

Spring Flowers

On her breakfast tray, Aunt Lily had a little vase of flowers—a mixture of primroses and celandines. She counted up the petals and found there were 39. "Oh, how lovely!" she said, "exactly my age; and the total number of flowers is exactly your age, Rose!"

How old is Rose?

Primroses have five petals on each flower.

Celandines have eight petals on each flower.

Sesquipedalian Farm

On an ordinary farm, if one goose lays one egg in one day, then you can easily work out how many eggs seven geese lay in a week, can't you? One goose lays seven eggs in a week; so seven geese lay seven times that many—that's 49 eggs a week.

But, on Sesquipedalian Farm things are a bit different, because a hen and a half lays an egg and a half in a day and a half (how very strange!) so how many eggs would seven hens lay in a week and a half?

Spring Flowers

The way to figure this out is to start at the end with 39 petals, and remember that the primroses must provide either 5 petals or 10 or 15 or 20 or 25 or 30 or 35—a multiple of 5. Now suppose there was only one celandine (8 petals); that would leave 31 petals (39 − 8 = 31). The rest can't be primroses, because 31 is not an exact multiple of 5. Suppose there were two celandines; that would make 16 petals, leaving 23. No good! Three celandines = 24 petals, and 39-24 = 15 petals. Bingo! The answer must be 3 celandines and 3 primroses. Check: 3 × 8 = 24 and 3 × 5 = 15, and 24 + 15 = 39. So Rosa is (3+3), or 6.

Three-Quarters Ranch

It's no surprise that calculations get even more compli-cated at Three-Quarters Ranch, where a duck and three quarters lays an egg and three-quarters in a day and three-quarters.

How many eggs do seven ducks lay in a week?

You will need a calculator for this trick. First secretly enter 271 and × or * to multiply. Then ask your friend what her favorite digit is, from 2 to 9. While she watches, punch it in, and press =. Then give her the calcula-tor, and tell her to multiply by 41, and see what she gets; all her own digits! To find out how this works, multiply 41 × 271 and see if you can figure it out.

Sesquipedalian Farm

If 1½ hens lay 1½ eggs in a day and a half,
then 1 hen lays 1 egg in a day and a half,
and 2 hens lay 2 eggs in a day and a half,
and 7 hens lay 7 eggs in a day and a half,
so 7 hens lay 14 eggs in three days,
so 7 hens lay 28 eggs in six days,
so 7 hens lay 42 eggs in nine days;
add what they lay in 1½ days
(+7) eggs in a day and a half),
so 7 hens lay 49 eggs in 10½ days, which is a week and a half.

Cookie Jars

Joe and Ken each held a cookie jar and had a look inside them to see how many cookies were left.

Joe said, "If you gave me one of yours, we'd both have the same number of cookies."

Ken said to Joe, "Yes, but you've eaten all yours, and you haven't any left!"

How many cookies does Ken have?

Three-Quarters Ranch

We know 1¾ ducks lay 1¾ eggs in 1¾ days. Imagine that we can replace 1¾ ducks by a special bird called a Megaduck.

Then we can say:

1 Megaduck lays 1¾ eggs in 1¾ days;
so 1 Megaduck lays 1 egg in 1 day;
so 1 Megaduck lays 7 eggs in 1 week.

Now, how many Megaducks are there in 7 ducks?
Answer 7 divided by 1¾, which turns out to be 4!
($4 \times 1 = 4$, and $4 \times \frac{3}{4} = 3$, and $4 + 3 = 7$).

The original question was, "How many eggs do 7 ducks lay in a week?" Since 7 ducks is the same as 4 Megaducks, and since each Megaduck lays 7 eggs in a week, 4 Megaducks lay $4 \times 7 = 28$ eggs a week. So, 7 ducks lay 28 eggs a week.

Fleabags

Two shaggy old dogs were walking down the street.

Captain sits down and scratches his ear, then turns to Champ and growls, "If one of your fleas jumped onto me, we'd have the same number."

Champ barks back, "But if one of yours jumped onto me, I'd have five times as many as you!"

How many fleas are there on Champ?

The Rolling Quarter

Imagine a quarter laid on the table and fixed there, perhaps with a dab of glue. Now lay another quarter against it, and roll the second quarter all the way around the first one, without any slipping at the edges, until it gets back to where it started.

In making one complete circuit, how many times does the second quarter rotate?

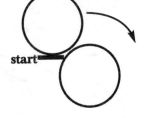

start

MATHBIT

Have you seen the patterns in the sevenths, when turned into decimals? Use a calculator to work out 1/7, 2/7, 3/7, and so on, and this is what you get:

1/7 =	0.14285714	285714	2857...
2/7 =	0.285714	285714	285714...
3/7 =	0.4285714	285714	28571...
4/7 =	0.57142	857142	8571428...
5/7 =	0.7142	857142	85714285...
6/7 =	0.857142	857142	857142...

SOLUTION

Fleabags

Captain has two fleas; Champ has four.

Sliding Quarters

Here's a puzzle that looks simple, but is really quite tricky. Even when you have seen the answer you sometimes can't remember it. Maybe you are smart enough to solve it on your own, but if you go on to baffle your friends, make sure you can remember the solution when you need it!

Lay six quarters on the table touching in two rows of three, like this:

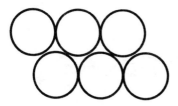

In each move, slide one quarter, without moving any others, until it just touches two others. In only three moves, can you get them into a circle like this?

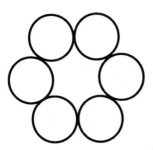

SOLUTION

The Rolling Quarter

Twice. Try it and see.

Picnic Mystery

Allie takes fruit, cake, and cookies for her picnic. She has three boxes for them. One is labeled FRUIT. One is labeled COOKIES. One is labeled CAKE. But she knows her Mom likes to fool her and has put every single thing in the wrong box. The only other thing she knows for sure is that the fruit is not in the CAKE box.

Where is the cake?

What digits do you get if you use a calculator to divide 100 by 81? Well, how about that! Try it and see!

Sliding Quarters

Practice this before you try to show anyone!

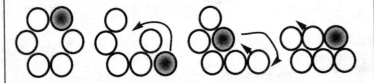

Pick up and use the dark quarter to move the other ones.

Find the Gold

Lucy Sly, a brilliant detective, has tracked some pirates to their island base. In their secret cave, she finds the pirate chief with three chests of treasure. One chest contains pieces of iron, one chest pieces of gold, and the third has a mixture.

In return for a chance to escape, the pirate chief offers Lucy one chest to take away with her. All three chests are labeled—IRON, GOLD, and MIXTURE. But, he warns her, all the labels are on the wrong chests.

"Then I can't tell which is which," she replies.

"I will take one object out of any one of these chests, and show it to you—although you may not look inside."

Which chest would you choose to see an object from? And how would you be sure you got the chest of gold?

Frisky Frogs

Across a stream runs a row of seven stepping stones.

On one side of the stream, sitting on the first three stones, are three girl frogs, Fergie, Francine, and Freda, and they want to get across to the other side.

There's an empty stone in the middle.

On the other side are three boy frogs, waiting to come across the other way—Fred, Frank, and Frambo.

Only one frog moves at a time. Any frog may hop to the next stone if it is empty, or may hop over one frog of the opposite sex on to an empty stone.

Can you get all the frogs across the river?

Leaping Lizards

Across a stream runs a row of eight stepping stones.

On one side of the stream, on the first five stones, sit five girl lizards–Liza, Lizzie, Lottie, Lola, and Liz–and they want to get across to the other side.

There's one empty stone in the middle.

On the other side are three boy lizards, waiting to come across the other way–Lonnie, Leo, and Len.

Only one lizard moves at a time. Any lizard may hop to the next stone if it is empty, or may hop over one lizard of the opposite sex onto an empty stone.

Can you get all the lizards across the river, and what's the smallest number of leaps?

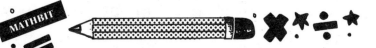

MATHBIT

Many spiders weave beautiful roundish webs, with a single strand spiraling out from the center. These amazing creatures keep the distances and turns so exact. Watch for webs on damp and frosty mornings and count the radial lines used in its construction.

Chewed Calculator

You look for your calculator to help work out some figures, and when you finally find it you can see that the dog has been chewing on it! He has chewed up all the number buttons, so that not one of them works, except for the 4.

What's more, the 4 button only seems to work if you press it four times, and then you get four 4s!

All of the other calculator keys work: (*) (/) (+) (–) (=) (sqrt) (MS) (MR) and (1/x), but strangely enough no other numbers.

How can you get all the numbers from 1 to 10 using only four 4s for each?

Examples:
  You can make 1 by punching in 4/4=*4/4=
  You can make 2 by punching in 4+4=MS4*4=/MR=

  Can you figure out how to make 3, 4, 5, and the other numbers up to 10?

Crushed Calculator

This time, you are shocked to find out that a small tame elephant has sat on your calculator! When you try to use it, you find that all the function buttons are working: (+) (–) (/) (*) (=) (sqrt) (1/x).

The memory is working, too, but all the number buttons are busted except for the 1, 2, 3, and 4.

Using only the working 1, 2, 3, 4 buttons. and using each of them once every time, can you make all the numbers from 1 to 20?

Examples:
  You can make 5 by punching 4*2=*1=-3=
  You can make 6 by punching 4/2=*3=*1=

Are you able to work out the others?
You need to be clever for this one.

Chewed Calculator

To make 3: 4+4+4/4= =3
To make 4: 4-4+4sqrt=+4sqrt= =4
To make 5: 4*4=+4=/4= =5
To make 6: 4+4+4/4sqrt= =6
To make 7: -4/4=+4+4= =7
To make 8: 4+4+4-4= =8
To make 9: 4/4+4+4= =9
To make 10: 4+4+4-4 sqrt= =10

Knot Me!

Find a piece of rope or string and lay it on a table. Then, pick it up with a hand at each end and, without letting go of the ends of the rope, tie a knot in the rope.

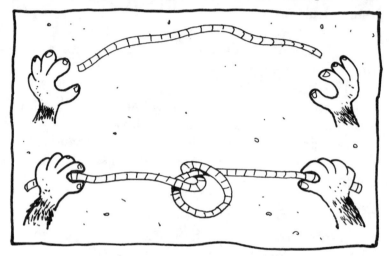

Can it be done? Yes it can. When you have figured out the secret, challenge your friends to knot the rope!

Crushed Calculator

To make 1: $1×2=+3−4 = 1$
To make 2: $4−3=×2×1= 2$
To make 3: $4−2−1=×3= 3$
To make 4: $4+3−2−1 = 4$
To make 5: $4+3−2×1 = 5$
To make 6: $4+3−2+1 = 6$
To make 7: $2−1=×4+3= 7$
To make 8: $1−2+3=×4= 8$
To make 9: $4×3=−2−1 = 9$
To make 10: $4×2=+3−1 = 10$

...and see how much further you can go!

Unknot Me!

Make a simple knot in the rope and lay it on the table.

Challenge your friends to pick it up with a hand at each end and, without letting go of the ends, make another knot that will untie the first. Is it possible?

MATHBIT

The Earth moves around the sun once a year in an orbit that's an ellipse, not a circle. Can you draw an ellipse? Sure. Tie a short piece of string into a small loop. Push two thumbtacks into a pad or cardboard, drop the loop over them, and draw. (Moving the tacks closer together makes a more circular ellipse; while moving them apart makes it thinner.)

SOLUTION

Knot Me!

When you pick up the rope, the rope, your arms, and your body all form a closed loop. It's mathematically impossible to create a new knot in a closed loop. So the only way to get a knot in the rope is to "knot your arms" before picking up the rope. Fold your arms first, then pick up the rope with one hand reaching over one elbow and one under the other elbow. Keeping hold of the rope, unfold your arms, and you transfer the knot to the rope.

Squares & Cubes

Multiply any number by itself, and you get a square number. So 2 x 2 = 4, and 4 is a square number. And four squares fit together to make a bigger square.

Nine is also a square, because 3 x 3 = 9, and nine squares also fit together to make a bigger square.

Cubes are numbers you get by multiplying a number by itself and then by the same again; so 2 x 2 x 2 = 8, which is a cube.

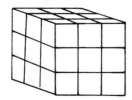

And 3 x 3 x 3 = 27, another cube. The big cube is made of 27 little cubes.

There is only one 2-digit number (i.e. between 10 and 99 that is both a square and a cube. What is it?

SOLUTION

Unknot Me!

It's impossible to untie a knot with another knot (you cannot tie an unknot!) Knots *always* add together. What you *can* do, although it may not be easy, is push your hands, while holding the rope ends, into the *loose* knot so that the knot is transferred back onto your now crossed arms! Simply reversing Knot Me!

Cubes & Squares

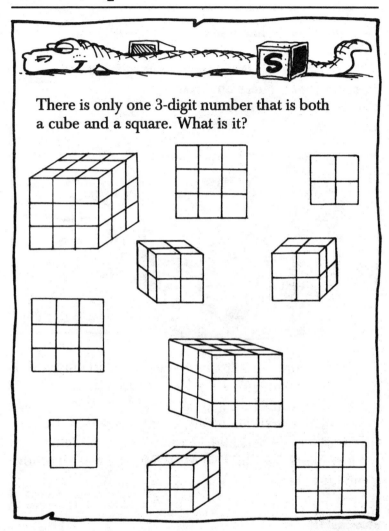

There is only one 3-digit number that is both a cube and a square. What is it?

SOLUTION

Squares & Cubes

$64 = 8 \times 8$ and $4 \times 4 \times 4$

Old MacDonald

Old MacDonald had a farm, EE-I-EE-I-OH!
And on that farm he had some pigs, EE-I-EE-I-OH!
With an *Oink oink!* here, and an *Oink oink!* there.
Here an *Oink!* There an *Oink!*
Everywhere an *Oink oink!*
Old MacDonald had a farm, EE-I-EE-I-OH!

Old MacDonald had some turkeys, too (certainly with a *Gobble gobble* here and a *Gobble gobble* there).

One day, while out feeding them all, he noticed that, if he added everything together, his pigs and his turkeys had a total of 24 legs and 12 wings between them.

How many pigs did Old MacDonald have? And how many turkeys?

Old Mrs. MacDonald

Mrs. MacDonald was a farmer too. She kept the cows and chickens. One day when she went out to feed them she counted everything up, and found that her animals had a total of 12 heads and 34 legs.

How many cows did she have? How many chickens?

MATHBIT

If you use a combination lock, you can easily work out how long it will take a thief to try all the numbers and open it. If it has four dials with 10 digits on each, then there are a total of 10,000 different combinations. If the thief takes one second to try each, it will take nearly three hours to go through every number, since in three hours there are $3 \times 60 \times 60$ seconds, or 10,800 seconds. On average, though, a thief will reach your secret number in half that time—say an hour and a half. (See MATHBIT on page 70.)

SOLUTION

Old MacDonald

All the 12 wings must have belonged to turkeys, because pigs don't usually have any; so he must have had 6 turkeys (with 2 wings each). The 6 turkeys must have had 12 legs, leaving 12 legs for the pigs, and since each pig has 4 legs, that makes 3 pigs. So Old MacDonald had 3 pigs and 6 turkeys.

Wiener Triangles

In the link-wiener factory in Sausageville, the wieners are made in long strings, with a link of skin holding each sausage to the next one. So, although the wieners are firm, you can bend the string of wieners around into many shapes. For example, you can easily bend a string of three wieners into a triangle.

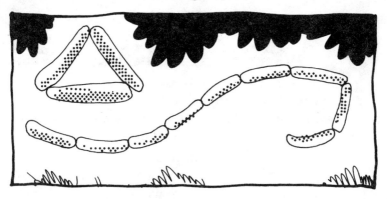

Suppose you had a string of 9 wieners. Without breaking the string, how many triangles can you make?

Old Mrs. MacDonald

Mrs MacDonald counted 12 heads, so she must have had 12 animals. If they had all been chickens she would have had 24 legs; if they had all been cows she would have had 48 legs.

The difference between these two is 24, or 2 legs more than 24 for each cow. She counted 34 legs. That is 10 more than 24; so she must have had 5 cows.

Check; 5 cows = 5 heads; 7 chickens = 7 heads;
total 5+7= 12 heads.

And 5 cows = 20 legs; 7 chickens = 14 legs;
total 20+14 = 34 legs.

Tennis Tournament

You successfully arranged a "knock-out" tennis tournament, in which the winners of the first round meet in the second round, and so on. The little tournament had only four players, so arranging it was easy.

In the first round, Eenie played Meanie, and Eenie won. Miney played Mo, and Mo went through to the second round. In the second round—the final—Mo beat Eenie, and won the tournament.

The 3-game match card looked like this:

1st round   2nd round   winner

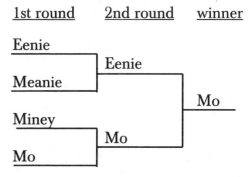

The match was so well organized, you've been asked to arrange another knock-out tennis tournament. This time 27 players enter. How many matches will have to be played to find the winner?

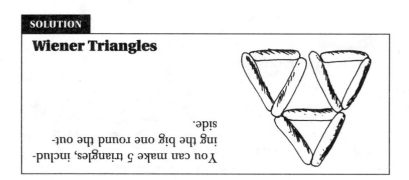

SOLUTION

Wiener Triangles

You can make 5 triangles, including the big one round the outside.

Magic Triangle

Here's a triangle of ovals:

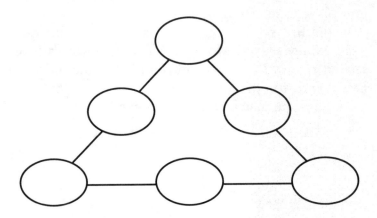

Can you write the numbers 1 through 6 in the circles, using each number once, so that the total you get by adding the numbers along each side always comes to 9?

Magic Hexagon

Here is a section of a honeycomb—seven hexagons in a group.

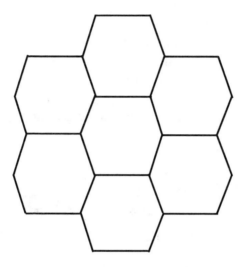

Can you write the numbers 1 through 7, one in each hexagon, so that all three lines across the middle add up to a total of 12?

SOLUTION

Magic Triangle

Now can you rearrange the same numbers so that each side totals 12?

59

House Colors

George and Greg Green both live with their families in big houses on Route 1, just outside town, and their sister Bernice, married to Bert Blue, lives in the third house on the same road.

One day, they all secretly decided to paint their houses the same color as their names, and were glad to find out afterwards that no next-door houses were the same color.

Who lives in the middle house of the three?

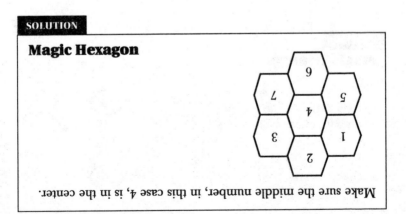

MATHBIT

How many people do you think need to be in a room before there is a fifty/fifty chance that two of them will have the same birthday?

Answer, only 23! Try it in your class.

SOLUTION

Magic Hexagon

Make sure the middle number, in this case 4, is in the center.

Three Sisters

Three sisters, Ady, Beady, and Cedie, went out into the wide world and found jobs; one of them became an architect, one a builder, and the third a cook. Then they married Mr Able, Dr. Baker, and Charlie. None of the first letters in their first and last names or occupations match up–so Mr Able is not married to Ady, and she is not the architect. If Charlie's wife isn't a builder, who married the doctor?

House Colors

Houses #1 and #3 must be green, because they are not next door to one another; so Bernice and her family live in the middle house.

LoadsaLegs

Two multipedes were dancing together at a party, and trying hard not to trip over each other's feet! One smiled at the other and said, "If you could give me two of your legs we'd have the same number." The other replied, "If I had two of yours, I'd have three times as many legs as you!"

How many legs did each have?

Three Sisters

Charlie's wife isn't the builder, and she isn't the cook (or the first letters would match); so she must be the architect, and she must be Beadie, or the first letters would match. Therefore Cedie can't be the architect or the cook; she must be the builder, and be married to Mr Able. And so the cook, married to Dr Baker, must be Ady.

Antennas

Two robots are strutting through cyberspace, trying to keep in touch with everything on the World Wide Web.

Abot says to Bbot, "I get such a headache trying to listen to all these radio signals at the same time. Do you know that if you gave me two of your antennas we'd have the same number?"

Bbot retorted "That's nothing! If I had two of your antennas I'd have five times as many as you!"

How many antennas does each of them have?

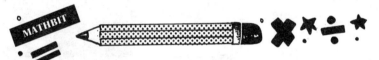

All numbers have factors, which divide evenly into them. The factors of 8 are 1, 2, and 4. Perfect numbers are special because they are equal to the sum of their factors. The number 6 is perfect because its factors are 1, 2, and 3, and their sum $1 + 2 + 3 = 6$. The next perfect number is 28, because it is the sum of 1, 2, 4, 7, and 14. The third perfect number is 496!

SOLUTION

LoadsaLegs

One had 6 legs; the other had 10.

The Power of Seven

Far back in history, a lonely fort was being desperately defended against thousands of attackers.

The attacks came regularly at noon every day, and the defending commander knew he had to survive only three more days, for then would come the end of the attackers' calendar, and they would all go home to celebrate, giving time for his reinforcements to arrive.

He also knew that the attackers held an unshakable belief in the power of the number seven. So he always placed seven defenders on each wall of the fort. With

three attacks to come, and only 24 defenders, he places 5 along each wall, and 1 in each corner tower.

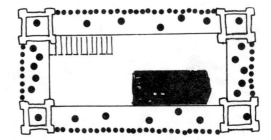

The attackers charge in from the north, and see seven defenders along that wall. Firing a volley of arrows, they wheel round and retreat, chanting "Neves! Neves!" meaning seven in their language. They charge from the west and again see seven defenders facing them. Firing a volley of arrows they retreat again. "Neves! Neves!"

From the south then the east, again they charge. Each time they are met by exactly seven defenders. Each time they turn and flee, chanting "Neves! Neves!" And the attack is over for the day.

SOLUTION

Antennas

Abot has 4 antennas; Bbot has 8.

The commander mops his worried brow as the bugle blows the bugle to signal "Well done and all clear!" Then he learns the arrows have killed four of his men.

How can he rearrange the remaining 20 so that by noon of the next day there will still be 7 defenders on each side?

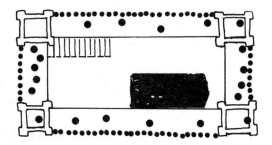

The Power of Seven continues

At noon on the second day the pattern of attack is different; the attackers come from the west, from the south, from the north, and then from the east. Each time they see seven defenders, fire a volley of arrows, and retreat, chanting "Neves! Neves!"

The attack is over, but five more men have been killed. Is it still possible for the commander to place seven defenders along each wall, now that he has only 15 altogether?

In other words, can they survive that third, final day of attack?

The Power of Seven

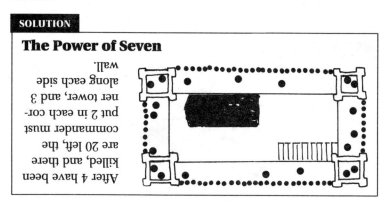

After 4 have been killed, and there are 20 left, the commander must put 2 in each corner, 3 in each tower, and 3 along each side wall.

Bundles of Tubes

William Posters set up a company to make cardboard tubes and sell them for the protection of large pictures or posters sent through the mail. He advertised:

> ## KEEP YOUR POSTERS SAFE WITH BILL POSTERS' TUBES!

He makes some tubes 2 inches in diameter and some 3 inches in diameter, for extra big posters. He sells the bigger tubes in bundles of 19, and the smaller tubes in bundles of 37.

Most people sell things in tens, or dozens, or even packets of 25. Why do you think he chose 19 and 37?

SOLUTION

The Power of Seven continues

Yes, they can survive the final attack. Four defenders go in one corner tower, three in all the others. 15 men make 7 on each side!

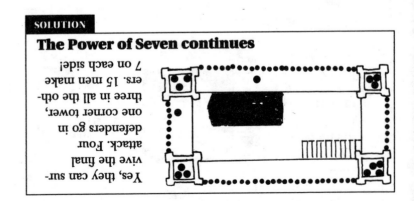

Pyramids

Susie and Ben like to make quick and easy cannonball cookies, so they often make lots and lots.

Today, they decide to heap the cookies up on the table for the family in pyramid shape.

Susie decides to make a triangular base with 6 cookies along each side, and builds up her pyramid from there–5 along each side in the next layer, then 4, then 3, and so on up to 1 on top.

Ben starts by laying out a square on the table, with only 5 cookies on each side. Then he builds up 4 on each side, then 3, and so on.

Which of the two pyamid builders uses more cookies by the time they reach the top?

Bundles of Tubes

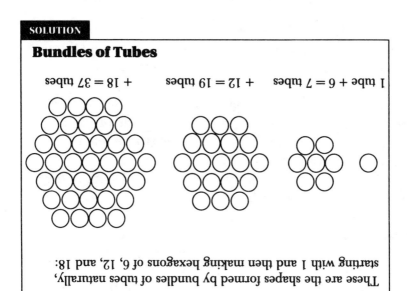

1 tube + 6 = 7 tubes + 12 = 19 tubes + 18 = 37 tubes

These are the shapes formed by bundles of tubes naturally, starting with 1 and then making hexagons of 6, 12, and 18:

Wrong Envelope?

You decide one day to write a letter to each of three friends. When you finish, you go to a desk and find three envelopes, write the address on each envelope, and stick on a stamp.

Now, suppose you were to put one letter into each of the envelopes without looking at the front of it, how many ways are there of putting at least one letter into the wrong envelope?

What is the chance that you will get the letters in the right envelopes just by luck?

SOLUTION

Pyramids

Susie needs 56 cookies; Ben needs 55.

1) Which 2-digit number is 1 more than a square, and 1 less than a cube?

2) Which three-digit number, made of consecutive digits, like 567, is 2 less than a cube and 2 more than a square?

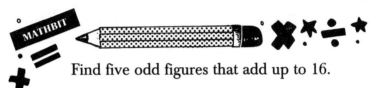

MATHBIT

Find five odd figures that add up to 16.

(Answer: 1 + 1 + 1 + 13.) When you try this on your friends, take care to say "figures" rather than "numbers," or the trick won't work!

SOLUTION

Wrong Envelope?

Think of the three envelopes as A, B, and C, and the three letters as a, b, and c. Then you can write down the six different ways of arranging the letters like this:

1	2	3	4	5	6
Aa	**Aa**	Ab	Ab	Ac	Ac
Bb	Bc	Ba	Bc	Ba	**Bb**
Cc	Cb	Ca	Cc	Cb	Ca

Only #1 has all the letters in the right envelopes; so there are five ways of putting at least one letter into the wrong envelope, and your chance of getting it all right just by luck is one in six. There are only two arrangements with all the letters in the wrong envelopes. Can you find any arrangements with two letters in the right envelopes and one wrong?

Good Neighbor Policy

Kind old Mrs. Werbenuik always liked to present her friends with special gifts during the holidays. One year she took pottery classes on Wednesday evenings and, while there, she made three fancy little pots. Later, she filled them with special homemade apple jelly, and gave them to her neighbors—a family of two fathers and two sons. They were very happy with their gifts.

How could the three pots of jelly be divided equally and fairly between two fathers and two sons?

What if the combination lock you have has only three digits, and they only go from 0 to 6? Then the total number of possible combinations is only 6 × 6 × 6 or 216, and a thief could very likely go through all those number to open the lock in less than four minutes!

Cutting the Horseshoe

Here's a picture of a horseshoe.

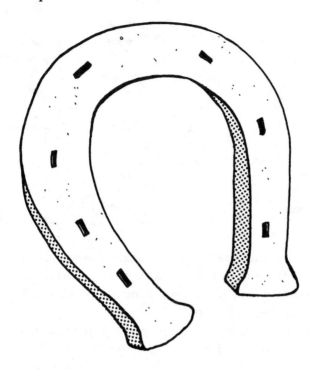

Your challenge is to cut it into seven pieces, each containing a nail hole, with just two straight cuts. After the first cut, you can put the pieces on top of one another, but both cuts have to be straight.

Can you make seven "holey" pieces?

Multisox

Two multipedes are cantering through a shopping mall, when they come to a sock shop. They count up all their feet and find that three dozen, or 36, socks will be just enough to keep all of their feet warm.

If one of them has eight feet more than the other, how many feet does each multipede have?

SOLUTION

Cutting the Horseshoe

First cut across both arms, leaving two holes below the cut on each side, to give three pieces. (Cut 1)

Pile these up so that your second cut snips each of the bottom ends in half, and cuts out the top section with one hole. (Cut 2)

You have seven holey pieces!

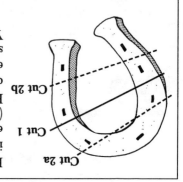

Three Js

Joan and Jane are sisters. Jean is Joan's daughter, and 12 years younger than her aunt.

Joan is twice as old as Jean.

Four years ago, Joan was the same age as Jane is now, and Jane was twice as old as her niece.

How old is Jean?

You can easily find if a big whole number can be divided by 3. Just add up the digits, and go on adding until you get only one digit. If that digit is a 3, 6, or 9, the larger number is divisible by 3; if not, not. So, try 12; $1 + 2 = 3$; 12 is divisible by 3.

256 $2 + 5 + 6 = 13$; $1 + 3 = 4$

256 is *not* divisible by 3

5846 $5+8+4+6 = 23$; $2+3=5$

5846 is *not* divisible by 3

7293654 $7+2+9+3+6+5+4 = 36$; $3+6=9$

7293654 *is* divisible by 3

Architect Art

Art became an architect,
    And thought he'd like to draw
        A house in three dimensions,
            But was not entirely sure
                That he could do it in one go,
                    And never lift his pen
                        Above the page, and not go o'er
                            Any line again.

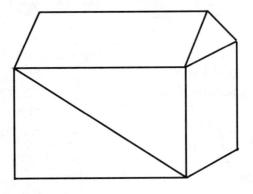

Can you do it? Can you draw this house with one continuous line, without lifting your pencil from the paper or going over any line twice?

(Hint: Start from a corner where an odd number of lines meet.)

No Burglars!

Worried by the number of burglaries in your town, you have just installed Fantastico High-Security Locks on all the doors in your house. They are so special that you actually have to walk through a doorway and lock the door behind you, and then it cannot be opened by anyone else.

Here is a plan of your house:

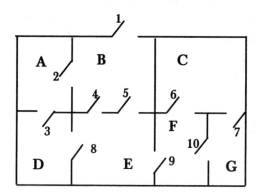

A = bedroom
B = hall
C = dining room
D = bathroom
E = living room
F = kitchen
G = den

You decide to go out to the movies. You need to go through and lock each door, ending with the front door.

In which room would you start? And in which order would you shut the doors behind you to make sure you went through and locked every one?

Train Crash

There's a single railroad track across the remote desert near the Arizona–New Mexico border. A freight train starts from one end and goes north at 25 mph. An ancient pioneer train starts at the other end and coughs its way south at a mighty 15 mph.

Neither driver sees the other train approaching, and at No Hope Gulch, after both trains have been traveling for exactly one hour, they collide head-on.

There's a lot of arguing about who's to blame, but the question is, How far apart were the trains when they started, exactly one hour before the crash?

Squished Fly

At the moment when the trains started up, a fly that had been sleeping on one locomotive woke up and took off.

Strangely enough, it flew straight up the line at 50 mph to the front of the other train! There, it turned right around and flew straight back to the freight train!

Again, it turned right around and flew *back* to the other train! Backwards and forwards the fly went, between the two trains, until at the bitter end—the fly was *squished* in the crash!

It's a long and strange story, but the question remains: How far did the fly fly, before it died?

Train Crash

In the hour before the crash one train must have traveled 25 miles, and the other 15. So one hour before the crash they were (25 + 15) or 40 miles apart.

Puzzle of the Sphinx

Here are four little sphinxes, small versions of the big one found in the Egyption desert.

How can you rearrange these four sphinx shapes to make one big sphinx?

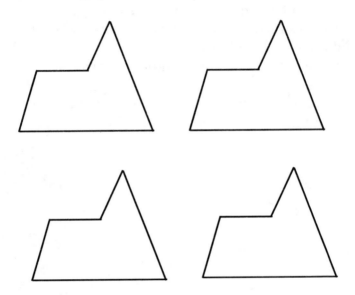

(Hint: It's really just a small jigsaw puzzle, except that one of the "pieces" fits in backwards.*)*

Perforation!

You have 12 postage stamps that have a picture of your favorite flower on each.

You want to put them in your stamp book, but it's made for 3 rows of 4 stamps like this, not 4 rows of 3.

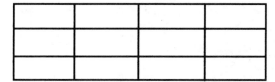

How can you tear the sheet of stamps, along the perforations, into only two pieces so that they will fit together and fill your page better?

SOLUTION

**Puzzle of
    the Sphinx**

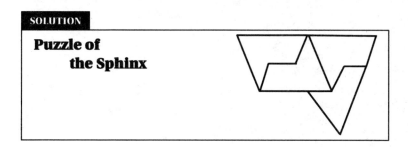

Heavibrix

A brick weighs a pound and half a brick.

How many pounds do two bricks weigh?

Perforation!

Tear the sheet in a zigzag pattern, starting from the left one stamp up from the bottom. Then slide the lower piece up to the right.

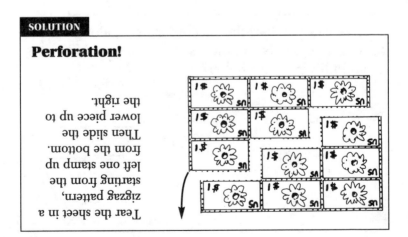

Disappearing Apples

Joe bought a bag of apples on Monday, and ate a third of them. On Tuesday he ate half of the remaining apples. On Wednesday he looked in his bag and found he had only two apples left.

How many did he have to start with?

In the late sixteenth century, the Italian scientist Galileo was gazing at a church lamp swinging to and fro and realized the time of each swing was always the same. Making pendulums by tying weights on various lengths of string, he discovered that when he doubled the string length, the swing of the pendulum took four times as long. How long would a pendulum take to swing if its string were three times as long?

Heavybrix

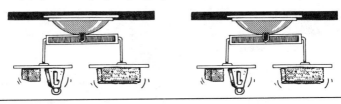

If a brick weighs a pound and a half a brick, then two bricks weigh 2 pounds and a brick.

So taking a brick away from each side, one brick weighs 2 pounds. So two bricks weigh 4 pounds.

Wild Geese

Aunt Rody has nine wild geese in a big square pen. The trouble is, they are so wild they keep fighting; so she decides to separate them all.

Where can she build two more square pens so that all the geese are separated?

SOLUTION

Bag of Apples

two the second.

He had six apples to start with, and ate two the first day and

Beefy Bison

In 1976, in honor of 200 years of American Independence (USA bicentennial), Aunt Rhody started a bison ranch, keeping 16 bison in a big field. She's kept the bison fenced-in in groups of 2, 3, 3, and 8. Now she wants to change it to groups of 4, 6, and 6.

How can she do this by moving only two fences?

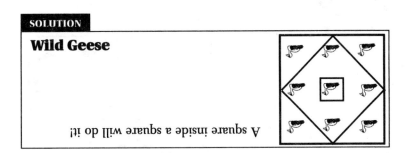

Wild Geese

A square inside a square will do it!

Colored Balls #1

You have five red balls,

five yellow balls,

and five blue balls.

How can you arrange them in this triangular frame so that no two balls of the same color are next to one another?

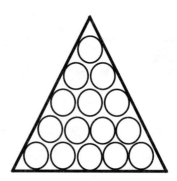

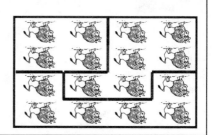

Colored Balls #2

You have six yellow balls

and four blue balls.

How can you arrange them in this triangular frame so that no three yellow balls make an equilateral triangle— a triangle in which all three sides are the same length?

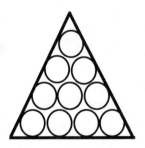

Colored Balls #1

85

Logical Pop

You have three identical cans. One is labeled POP, one is labeled MILK SHAKE, and one is labeled POTATO CHIPS.

However, you know your mischievous sister has, as a joke, changed all the labels, so that every label is on the wrong can.

You want to open the pop, but you are allowed to open only one can; so you have to get it right.

To get a clue, you may shake one can first. Which one would you shake, and how would you choose which can to open?

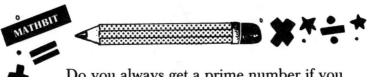

Do you always get a prime number if you multiply a number by the next number and then add 17? For example $6 \times 7 = 42$, add 17 makes 59, which is a prime number.

SOLUTION

Colored Balls #2

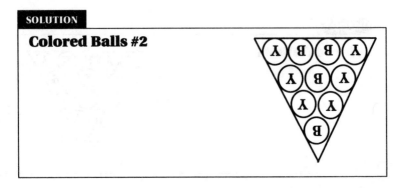

Pool of Glue

When the teacher Miss Take comes into her second grade classroom, she is about to sit down when she sees a pool of glue on her chair.

There are only three girls in the room, Pansy Potter, Peony Plummer, and Petal Prancer, and there is no way anyone else could have left the room. So one of the three must have put the glue there.

Miss Take immediately questions the three girls:

Pansy Potter says, "It was Peony that poured the glue on your chair!"
Peony Plummer says, "No; it was Petal!"
Petal Prancer says, "I didn't do it!"

Two of the girls are telling the truth, but one is lying. Who is the guilty one?

Logical Pop

You should shake either the can labeled MILK SHAKE or the can labeled POP. The potato chips must be in one of those two cans, and they should rattle.

Suppose you shake the MILK SHAKE can; if it rattles it contains the chips; the pop must be in the can labeled POTATO CHIPS. If it doesn't rattle, it must contain the pop.

Meanwhile if you shake the POP can and it rattles, the chips must be in it; so the milk shake must be in the can labeled POTATO CHIPS, which means the pop must be in the MILK SHAKE can. If it doesn't rattle, the pop must be in the can labeled POTATO CHIPS.

How Many Ducks?

Little Francine saw some ducks going through a gap in the hedge and out into the field. She had never seen any ducks before; so she was excited by the little procession.

When she told her aunt about them later, her aunt asked how many ducks she had seen.

"Well," said Francine, "I'm not much good at counting, but there was a duck in front of a duck and a duck behind a duck and a duck in the middle."

What is the smallest number of ducks she could have seen?

MATHBIT

The equals sign $=$ was invented in 1557 by Welsh mathematician Robert Recorde. In his book, *The Whetstone of Witte*, he wrote "to avoid the tedious repetition of these words: is equal to; I will set *a pair of parallel lines* thus, $==$, because no two things can be more equal."

SOLUTION

Pool of Glue

Peony says it was Petal; Petal says it was not. These two statements claim opposite things; so one of them must be true and one must be a lie.

Since two of the girls are telling the truth, the third statement—Pansy's—must be true. So Pansy is telling the truth, which means that Peony did it.

Upending the Cups

Make yourself a row of seven plastic cups or mugs or paper water cups, all turned upside-down on the table.

The challenge is to turn them the right way up, but always turning over three at a time. So after your first turn they might look like this:

...or like this:

How can you turn them all the right way up, in just three goes?

Diluting the Juice

George the greenhorn gardener has just invested in four pints of the best organic fertilizer; green, glutinous, and gorgeous. Just the stuff to give those tender young plants.

The instructions on the brimming packet say "Before use, dilute with 2 pints of water."

George has a jug that holds 3 pints, and an old milk carton that holds 2 pints. He has no other containers.

How can he dilute the fertilizer, from his garden tap, in exactly the 2:1 ratio the packet says?

MATHBIT

The great mathematician G. H. Hardy went to visit his brilliant student Ramanujan in a hospital. Not having much to talk about, Hardy said "I came here in a taxi, #1729; not a very interesting number." Ramanujan heaved himself up from his sick bed, protesting "On the contrary, my dear Hardy, 1729 is a most interesting number. It's the smallest number that can be expressed as the sum of two cubes in two different ways!" ($1729 = 12\times12\times12 + 1\times1\times1$ and $1729 = 10\times10\times10 + 9\times9\times9$)

Puzzling Sand

Builder Bill needs exactly 11 pounds of sand to mix with cement, but when he goes to the sand supplier he is presented with a puzzle. The supplier has plenty of sand, and two big boxes on a balance, but he has only two weights: a 4-pound weight and a 5-pound weight.

He tells Bill, "If you can weigh out exactly 11 pounds into one of the boxes, without taking any sand out of either, you can have your sand for free!"

Bill puzzled and puzzled, and started pouring sand. Suddenly he saw how to do it.

What did he do?

Diluting the Juice

There are various ways to do this accurately. The neatest is to fill the 2-pint carton with fertilizer, then tip those 2 pints into the 3-pint jug, and fill it to the brim with water from the tap. The jug is then properly diluted, and can be poured straight on the garden. Then pour the remaining 2 pints from the packet into the 3-pint jug, and again fill it with water to dilute the rest of the fertilizer.

Secret Number Codes

To send a secret message to a friend, send the message in code so that no one else can read what it says. Of course, your friend needs to know how to decode the message, so only the two of you will understand.

This simple code changes each letter to a number:

A	B	C	D	E	F	G	H	I	J	K	L	M
1	2	3	4	5	6	7	8	9	10	11	12	13

N	O	P	Q	R	S	T	U	V	W	X	Y	Z
14	15	16	17	18	19	20	21	22	23	24	25	26

To send the message MEET ME AT SIX you write down their numbers instead of the letters:

13 5 5 20   13 5   1 20   19 9 24

But clever people might be able to guess this code, so you might want to make yours a little more complicated. See if you can work out what this message means:

14 6 6 21   14 6   2 21   20 6 23 6 15

(Hint: This second code is just a bit harder than the one above.)

SOLUTION

Puzzling Sand

Bill put the 5-pound weight in one box and balanced it with sand. Then he took the weight out, and balanced the sand with 5 pounds of sand in the other box. Then he put the 5 pound weight on top of the sand in one box, and the 4 pound weight in the other, and balanced up; so now one box had 6 pounds of sand, and the other 5. Finally he took both weights out, and put the 5 pound weight on top of the six pounds of sand. Then when he had balanced that, he knew he had exactly 11 pounds of sand.

92

Shape Code

This code looks much more mysterious. By using a shape instead of a number to stand for each letter, the same message—MEET ME AT SIX—looks so weird you might think it has no meaning at all. It doesn't even look like any kind of language, yet it's marvelous but simple code. Here's how to use it.

Make a grid and write in the letters as shown:

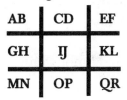 

Each space stands for one of the letters that was in it. The first letter of the two is shown by just the space; the second letter is shown by the space with a dot in it.

For A you write ⌐| for B you write •⌐|

for C you write ⌐⌐ for D you write ⌐•⌐

Now, can you figure out this message?

Sweet Spot

This is the toughest puzzle in the book. If you can solve it without peeking, you are a genius.

Windy, Wendy, and Woody sat in a triangle, facing one another. Their teacher said the brightest could have a candy bar. "I have here three white spots, and two black ones. I shall put one spot on each of your foreheads, so that you can see the others' spots, but not your own. The first to tell me what color you are, and how you know, wins the candy."

Then he stuck a white spot on each of their foreheads, making sure none of them could see any spots except those on the two heads.

After a minute, Wendy stood up. "I'm a white spot!"

"Sure?"

"Sure I'm sure."

How did Wendy know?

Solution on page 96.

...I'M SEEING SPOTS!...

Shape Code

The coded message is PHONE ME SOON.

Index

Page key: puzzle, **solution**.

MATHBITS

SOLUTION

Sweet Spot

Wendy said to herself, "Suppose I'm a black spot." Now, think about what Windy sees *if Wendy is black*. He sees one black spot and one white. He thinks, "If I were black, then Woody would see two black spots, and would know he was white." But Woody has not jumped up; so this cannot be true; Windy cannot be black. So Windy must know that he is white. But Windy has not jumped up and said so. Therefore Wendy's first guess must be wrong; Wendy cannot be black; so she *knows* she is white—and being the quickest to figure it out, she deserves to win the candy.